# Edge *by* Edge

# Edge *by* Edge

Gladys Justin Carr

Heidi Hart

Emma Bolden

Vivian Teter

POEMS

toadlily press
chappaqua, ny

Toadlily Press
P.O. Box 2, Chappaqua, NY 10514
www.toadlilypress.com

**Edge by Edge** © 2007 Toadlily Press
The Quartet Series

Cover Art: Detail from *MELD* by Elizabeth Levin
Cover photograph by Larry Goodman
Book Design by Liz Lester

The following poems have appeared or will appear in the publications cited:

"Across the Street All Autumn" *Spoon River Poetry Review;* "After the Fire Experiments" *The Gettysburg Review;* "Another Garden" *Worcester Review;* "Apocalypto" *FULCRUM: A Magazine of Poetry and Aesthetics;* "The Attempted Speaks" as "The Attempted Suicide Speaks" *Eclipse;* "Augustine's Brain—the Remix" *Diner: A Journal of Poetry;* "The Bench" *Eureka Literary Magazine, Meridian Anthology of Contemporary Poetry, Riverwind;* "Cherubim," *The Salt Flats Annual;* "Childhood" *Worcester Review;* "Door Psalm" *Monkscript;* "Eleanor of Aquitaine in the Winter of Her Discontent" *Salamander;* "End of the Affair" *Borderlands: Texas Poetry Review;* "The Established Household" *The Comstock Review;* "every Spark is numbered" *Poetry East;* "Her Face Became a Garden" *POEM, Meridian Anthology of Contemporary Poetry, Freshwater;* "Horse Chestnut Harvest" *The Salt Flats Annual;* "Hunger of No Tongue" and "Last Dance" *Green Mountains Review;* "In Ordinary Time" *Irreantum;* "Meditation on 'Tok,' the Dinka Word for 'One' " *Toowomba Refugee and Migrant Center Newsletter, Queensland, Australia;* "Personals" *Carquinez Poetry Review, Apalachee Review, Sanskrit Literary-Arts Magazine;* "Petition to the Fourth Dimension" *POEM, Schuylkill Valley Journal of the Arts;* "A Premise of Blue" *Karamu;* "Red-Winged Blackbird" *Poetry East;* "Ships" *Pebble Lake Review, Iodine Poetry Magazine;* "Slowing the Song" *Irreantum;* "Those in the Photos" as "Those in the Windows" *Black Warrior Review;* "Two Last Reasons for Words" as "Four More Reasons for Words" *Poetry East;* "Water Poem in a Time of War" *The Salt Flats Annual;* "X" *Cranky.*

PUBLISHER'S CATALOGING-IN-PUBLICATION DATA

Edge by edge : poems / Gladys Justin Carr . . . [et al.].
      p.   cm.   — (Quartet series)
     A collection of poems written by Gladys Justin Carr, Heidi Hart, Emma Bolden, and Vivian Teter.
    ISBN-13: 978-0-9766405-2-3
    ISBN-10: 0-9766405-2-X
    1. American poetry—21st century. I. Carr, Gladys Justin. II. Title.
    PS617 .E34   2007
    811.608             2007903420

# CONTENTS

EMMA BOLDEN
*How to Recognize a Lady*

VIVIAN TETER
*Translating a Bridge*

# FOREWORD

Maybe it's true that, as Tomas Tranströmer suggests, we can think of poems as meeting places, places where a connection is made and we're surprised into recognizing ourselves and the world. *Edge by Edge* is a terrific example of what Tranströmer has in mind—it sets four very active and impassioned voices in motion, and it asks us to let those voices pass through us as they travel toward each other. They air us out and enrich our oxygen, and we're all the more alive for it.

Gladys Justin Carr works with a metaphysical verve in her poems, a delightfully quick-witted intelligence full of steep angles and collaged fragments. Check out the piece called "Childhood," a masterful summary of growing up to recognize your own essential strangeness staring up at you from framed photos and family albums, "the tastes and smells of my green/life . . . fitted and frozen." She wants us to know that the surprises surviving inside of adult life are a kind of reward. The gifts of the earth are in music and singing especially, but all is in motion, unstable. "Say chaos theory collides/with the fact/of enchantment," she writes. So Carr is capable of addressing the fourth dimension (time), of referencing both Eleanor of Aquitaine and Dolly Parton, of making a remix of St. Augustine's thinking (one that somehow includes Wallace Stevens), and of somehow collapsing the distance between Odysseus and Sandy Koufax in roughly six lines. Her energy, though, has at its center a hard-won moral sensibility. Always.

Heidi Hart shares this strong moral sensitivity with Carr (as do the other poets). One of the wonderful things about her work is her calm in the face of the losses that death and suffering bring. Hart's calm is peculiar, it feels like the equanimity one gets to in reading the great haiku masters Bashō and Issa—the strength of being present, accepting. It feels like an invitation to friendship, the consolations of dailiness and its possibilities; and she grieves quietly "to think of snapping free from what may be/ the only heaven, here." Hart is concerned with how we all live now, a three-year-old naked and muddy and holding a flower blossom no less than "a Jewish mother and a Palestinian/whose son and brother had been lost/to gunfire." Our losses and hardships are ours to do something with. "Tell me," she says, invoking the image of Frances of Assisi, "what will you do with your secret poverty?" She asks both us and herself. Her answers are touching.

Emma Bolden casts the most satiric shadow of all these poets—her humor is more cutting and more often present as a weapon, a weapon aimed at the notion that it's enough for a woman merely to be a "good girl," perfect and selfless. Her subject is desire, and what it does to us—the good, the bad, and the ugly—the endlessness of wanting. Her music is deft and variable. Sometimes she achieves a Berryman-like comedy with it: "Bedsheets curdled, the night came down/nearer and dearer (my God) for he, a snore/beside me, bored already." And she has a gift for marrying music and perception mid-air: "eggshell shards fished/from a yolk's yellow eye." Beyond her humor, Bolden's honesty makes for a clear-eyed recognition of hurt—an uncomfortable hurt to be sure, but part of being alive, of wanting. Her poems are not weighted by this honesty though, thanks to their wildness of imagination and their fierce ironies (you have to love someone who could admit that she wishes Goldilocks had been eaten!).

Of the four poets gathered here, Vivian Teter is at once the most private in imagination and the one most drawn to address a world endangered by tribal warfare, mass graves, and globalized sweatshops, "the desperate red whip of the ache of this time." Her poems are moving in their insistence on vulnerability as a power. "To walk weaponless and unafraid" is what she might want to have her tattoo say, if she were interested in advertising her beliefs. She doesn't have to; she lives inside them. At the center of Teter's collection are two poems about the Lost Boys of southern Sudan. Like a number of her other poems, these are risky in their mood of prophetic outrage at betrayal and violence—it works for her because she makes it sound oddly intimate, the speech of one talking quietly and openly (and not on a soapbox). Teter is not a political poet, but her spiritual hunger often takes place against the backdrop of a political world. Her affection is for all that sweetness of being she knows exists in both people and nature, "that letter first opened long ago/then folded close at heart."

So here it is then, a meeting place—enter, and be welcome. Be changed.

David Rivard
*Cambridge, May 2007*

*Augustine's Brain—The Remix*

Gladys Justin Carr

# Augustine's Brain—The Remix

say there is knowledge
in a mystic's palm
invention in the membrane

⁂

say chaos theory collides
with the fact
of enchantment

⁂

say armies of past lives
march in the detritus
of fallen cities

⁂

say we tumble from grace
while birds blow by
& the emperor of ice cream sings

⁂

say these night words
make a crown of stars
to steer by

⁂

say what is written
is stained by the rose
of Augustine's brain

⁂

say we are paradox of laughter
& desolation      *gran partita*
of life's infinite jest

⁂

say we are ravished by a Jew's harp
scalded by desire
the cello in the heart

# The Bench

Out of silence, she,
wrapped smartly, brightly
scarved, shawled

may I sit here?
so elegant, so Act II
(the first being childhood

now this chance meeting
on a bench in middle age)
of course, he, pulling out his list

(and his heart) of things
he will talk about: oysters
molluscs, *papillons,* autumn rain

pebbles, pine woods, tumbling
in thickets, arthritis in the syntax
phrases like calculus of mushrooms

delectation of frogs, forgive me
I am negligent (*nec legere* →
not fitting well)

overheated by slanting atoms
of sun and rectitude
how careless of me

are you hungry? there's some Kierkegaard
in the fridge, she, laughing
are you a madman or a poet?

her arms fill with white orchids
tuberoses, birds of paradise
he inhales the fragrance

of her words he can barely
hear, his are torn, curled
in rags and swags of syllables

chatter he cannot stop
adjectives crashing
roiled ifs and buts

she in lowercase asks
(if he reads her right)
may I warm my hands

in your pockets? of course,
but beware of slugs, scamps,
demons, poppycock, pride

a pencil or two
and a few
small infamies

she, smiling, takes his hand
and the pocket fossils
of his years

# Her Face Became a Garden

*for the Central Park jogger*

Her face became a garden
    a nest for birds
*con amore ma non troppo*
    carved thigh-high
footprints stalked the grassy arms
    where hostas & anemones
stood guard in requiem line-up
    silent as the branches
laying hands upon her throat,
    her song.
Morning    sudden light    a still pool
    of roseblood
something wild stirs
    a scream
a bird    a prayer
    she runs again
through the forest    free
    yet trapped in time
between sleep and destiny
    her future overgrown
with wings
    that cannot fly.

# Eleanor of Aquitaine
# in the Winter of Her Discontent

watching

the sea

remembering
how it was

how we were

depraved by fits & starts
conjuring the wasp in the west

the sweet hummingbird
crabgrass & clay earth to suck
between the teeth
forgive me
I should speak of
feathers, lilies, Byzantium
next Friday's liturgy

here

this water vase is our vessel
catch the rain when it comes
catch the silence
in the wave
its clarity

once we were emperors
of clarity
ceramica
glyphs
now we are weapons
killers of the dream

still
I am love

arrest me
I endure

in the wave
in the silence

# Childhood

*après Dolly Parton*

I run from you    don't know you anymore
you're a fake    a fable    we sat around the table
laughed at cousin Lil who wasn't
getting married after all to tall & handsome
Bill    what to do about the pregnancy
nobody knew    we laughed at uncle Lou's
funeral too    nice man but god he looked
awful    like an orphan in that pink satin
coffin    someone shaved his mustache
that was wrong    pepper and salt
were passed    everyone ate peas and corn
but me    I threw up    stands to reason
in that young season the longest days held
light    rain as it ended dropped petals
like pearls in plain sight at my feet
I filled up with joy and ran
with the boys all the way back
from summer    couldn't catch up
so I joined the choir instead and made a sound
wild and wonderful like some loon on the lake
crazy with moon glow    that's when I began
to make tunes in my head
until the tastes and smells of my green
life seemed to get fitted and frozen
in pewter frames and gorgeous amber
albums opened    closed    opened again
up and down the ages
in those pages it looks like you
but I don't know you anymore
goes my song so I run from you
toward you    the dance of memory
the jig's up    it's not your face
but it's someone's face
I used to be

# Petition to the Fourth Dimension

now that we bring to world's end
    this clutch of felonies
        please
suspend sentence
    search the engines
        of mercy
pity these songs
    to your radiant
        silver dusting down
of ordinary time
    forgive us our forgeries
        imitations of love
lunatic infractions
    throw open your wings
        take us from this jail
hold us like new-born laughter
    in the rapture of your feathered hand
        so we become
what we are not yet
    before life
        and after

# Personals

**1.**

Looking for a post-structural feminist
Pop Rocker with traces of Woolf & Marjorie
Morningstar. Me? I'm just a has-been kind of guy
drunk on the good old B's (Burroughs, Beckett, Bukowski)
and an occasional C (Celine) with a Tinkers to Evers to
Chance love of background music (Mahler to Mozart
to The Grateful Dead). A hopeless romantic
y'know *Ich Liebe* this *Ich Liebe* that
Call me.

**2.**

Have you ever made love to a homeless person?
You do not have to blow me with your
kindnesses. No name no lineage. I offer you
my copy of Bashō & a six-pack of OutKast.
Hobbies: looking through windows without rooms,
listening to the ticking ticking ticking,
leaning into time . . .
You've got my number.

**3.**

When I love I sleep poorly so, criminal,
do not infect me, astound me, bruise me.
*(the longing for the dance stirs in the buried*
*life)* I am gentle as death, I cudgel
dead lovers to my breasts. Of course
I could kill you with my tiny knives
that glow like fireflies but there are so many
other ways to say I love you.
Try e-mail.

## Another Garden

*after Anne Carson*

You can find it only if you walk through

the season of flame when Sirius rises

a time of scorching heat     boys burn

but girls, mysteriously, thrive     the dog star

parches men's knees while tricky-minded

women laugh, their teeth tear out the hearts

of ripe melons, pulp of plums and passion

fruit     here, past Eve & Adam's place,

hemlock poured by Eros in a snaky suit

sluices down the aloe tree and warm

golden apples are on special today

# A Premise of Blue

cerulean, azure, whatever your name
don't come in the guise of Maeterlinck's
bird to swoop down the throat
of Gershwin's rows     I know you
anthracite dreams gone amok
your pretty Picasso blue jazz eyes
vamping Celine's agit rage that burns
cobalt holes in the night     you
dressed in your hues of funk
all veined up track-marked iambic
lines coming to me at 4 A.M.
like a pretend lover, chimera
seducer     don't give me that
robin's egg spring stuff that sweet
breath of lavender bullshit scent
of sea foam dying on Lalique shores
painted in bluest lies
like you, indigo     I see you
running     joystick thief
ink-stained     something wild
& red     my youth
in your teeth

# End of the Affair

Here, from your letter

    of departing leaves

a page of summer

    reads like Proust

with a whiff of madeleine

    so to speak

no need to speak

    silence is better

shattered by silence

    stay, light a lamp

there is time enough

    to inhabit dust

we are not yet done

    though the sun falls away

and windows fire

    red all over

# Ships

*after Czesław Miłosz*

one by one the ships
depart, my former lives, leaving

together with their sunsets

off to seas beyond dreaming

it is you, late autumn
rapture of another year

new birth come to mooring
your lights like pale fires

hang on ropes of night

now you must be my steel
steady craft against the wheel

of time     stay awhile

the icy lake will take us

soon enough

# Apocalypto

1.

Welcome, Prisoners
    it isn't the place you thought it would be
        after the galactic pop
                piffle, wisp,
                spit & small
                    fires

    nominal ice turds
        what once were cobblestones
if this be meltdown
    where's the bathtub gin—ask
        the phantoms eating charred potatoes
                in the fields
                of tides
    (they tell stories), shout down
        the drowners on Interstate 10
visit the coastlines that hang like shelves
    of continental drift

2.

row your boats to find missiles & monuments
    but do not go gently
        down that stream
mercury is risen
    fueling a new sun
here comes the avalanche of history
    dreamers, heroes, scamps,
                scalawags
                the carpetbaggers
                    of knock-offs
                    snake-oil charmers

the trickle-down gang
from the tear in God's eye

3.

malachite hearts with your irregularities
of pulse and pride    listen look
mountains are sprouting like broccoli
clowns, applaud
refugees, ride the Trojan Horse
to a replay of Eve's garden
spin the loop
called Fifties
pop fly out of the field to another screen
Brooklyn, say, in the time of our Lord
Koufax

4.

there they go, the Tribe of Will, the wretched
of the Earth, the Poets, note the lovely
trajectory of their renewal, how riots
are becalmed
by their villanelles
and a scruple
or two
are all the virgins lined up?
listen to their laughter
as they lash themselves to the beat
of the sea
Well done, Conscripts
this week's menu features
the passion of the fandango
Keep dancing
you who have
survived

*In Ordinary Time*

Heidi Hart

## Slowing the Song

Cricket song played back
at half and half again its ordinary speed
spreads into major thirds, a full-voiced triad choir

singing in circles, the same song for millennia.
Medieval churchmen thought this sound
too bright for the grim business of salvation;

how the major scale—to them, Ionian—
would grate like insects chafing with desire,
song as forbidden as the devil's interval from F to B,

song suspect in its innocence, the echo
of a lullaby, a child's taunt in a stableyard,
song not fit for Eden-fallen ears.

I never loved the major scale until
I heard the crickets sing its triads slow, not melody
but trinity in waves, arriving endlessly.

The cricket I find in my basement, one wing
broken after recent ambush by the cat,
has not been dropped from grace's garden.

It sang once. It suffers, as we want and wound
and sing the only songs we know,
calling to each other in the dark.

# Cherubim

The morning of the funeral, our maple fills with monarchs
heading north from Mexico. We stand with bare feet deep
in blossom litter, the same blooms the sticky bodies cling to,

orange-scaled, poison wings all shuttering, and every time
a car rolls by, the tree bursts open. My sons chase the thousand
wings until the angel folds its multiplicity into the leaves

and sleeps. After the funeral we hear a chopper's grinding
heartbeat overhead, mission unknown, already vanishing,
as my grandfather will swerve into my dreams

still wondering how God made the praying mantis,
his mind still out of reach, his body underground,
the word I longed to hear from him already flown.

# Horse Chestnut Harvest

*There are nothing but gifts on this poor, poor earth.*
CZESŁAW MIŁOSZ

To spare the neighbors' barefoot children

I put on my leather gloves and gather
this year's nuts still shiny from the cups

that held them until they broke open
in the branches of our century-old tree
that casts its gifts at us, from chandeliers of blossom

in the spring to this unwanted harvest and
the shedding of each broad, slick leaf. The world
grows plural, multiple, and doesn't seem to
tire, even this late in our tree's life, fall after fall.

My gloves scoop up another handful, brushing
soil where too much shade has kept
the grass from growing. The chestnuts smell
like childhood. How I used to hoard the ones
I found in the back gully, kindergarten afternoons,

and how they rolled out of my palm as hard as I
tried to hold on. I roll these into one tall grocery bag
and then another. Too much to carry in one load.
I want to take some to the friend who threatened
to jump from her balcony last week. There's enough
falling in the world, good seeds, this poison harvest,

all of it the world we know, and so I grieve
to think of snapping free from what may be
the only heaven, here.

## Lightning, Fireworks

Heaven's low tonight. And
    touches down. Could kill.
        Explosions in the street.
           A couple with a dog and
flashlight walk bent-backed.
    Searching the grass. For what—
        the woman's hands over her
           mouth—a ring? Or coins
bright as the moon? In her room, a widow wakes.
    Could swear the light's touched her as he
        would. Visiting. And gone.

# The Sunset Poem You Wanted

*after Robert Hass*

*Striated*, you say.
*Better than language,* I answer.
In the gallery, the famous poet
will soon speak of reading farmers' minds
in winter. Furrowing.

> Latin: *stria*
> Runnel in the barley field,
> hard to tell the water from the grain, the sky
> from channels in the mind.

We keep stopping. *Look—*
*between the branches—*

> Striated muscle fiber. Lava flow.
> Creekbed rock. The veins that radiate
> inside the skull, their rutted paths.

Soon we'll hear the famous poet's words
of reading a scored abstract canvas
and a Berlin diary: women's bodies split
by Russian soldiers who expected, after,
conversation.

> These empty branches:
> how they hold the edge of earth,
> bleeding as it turns.

# The Magic Hour

just after dawn or
right before dusk hoods the world

the hour when sky shows its gold
underside with bedroom lamps or
headlights on

the hour the filmmaker
prefers, when shadows slide away and
every face becomes
beloved

the hour of matins, vespers, virgin
body entered without breaking,
not by force but grace, the stained
glass window turned to wine

the hour we stand in protest
as the earth tips into
blindness, war across the world,
our hands suspended in each others'
hands, remembering

a quote we can't attribute:
*each of us holds light, but none*
*is spared some of the darkness,*
as we talk of thin red lines and blue
lines running through the heart,
between order and chaos, good

and ill, our very blood that changes
color when it breaks the skin;
we straddle federal property and sidewalk,
between the day and dark,
beloved, briefly, in the gap that does not
close and never will, as passing traffic
searches us with light

# In the Garden

*for Kate*

A string of summer lights. The wood roses
have fallen open. Paper garland in
the oak tree, wedding debris, the party
gone. Near our chairs, a fountain spills

and drains and spills. You're reading about
Schubert's last songs while I'm studying
his final string quartet's *Andante,* minor
third that roots itself in place, over

and over, and won't yield to changing harmony.
Next to us, a plaque reads *Friendship is
a plant of slow growth.* Yes. We'd give it
generations if we could. Already

crows are circling and pale spiders dropping
from the pine boughs. Fern fronds burn.

# Angel of History/ Book with Wings

*after two sculptures by Anselm Kiefer*
*Washington, D.C.*


not a holy book to eat in secret

but a broken spine/
a bomber made of storm

and leaves of lead
and poppies (dead)

too soft for flight
in this city thick with planes
from foreign wars hung lovingly
in the museum

in the city where you don't know who
is visitor and
who is plainclothes officer

until two interrogate a German tourist
*You heard the alarm*
*You didn't leave the building*
*Why*

and siren-call over the Capitol
sings to us to remember
everything

# In Ordinary Time

Miles from the flood-city where the dead drift out
into the street through open windows,

what sky shows through mine is darkening
to Dickensian soot. A hammer rings:

my boys have banded with their friends
to build a wood scrap fort against the looming rain,

against the TV images of a stampede
in Baghdad, bodies billowing along the Tigris.

Here in this more recent desert settlement, fresh
with faith in God and progress, plum trees swing

with unasked-for abundance, each windfall fruit a gift
or waste, who knows. I can hear my neighbors

talking prophecy—Old Testament—as rain
pulls at their kitchen screens. Another neighbor

belts her daughter's name until the thunder
takes her voice. So our epoch nears its end;

so have others; we're flotsam, I'm thinking
as my doorbell sounds its electronic carol and

I light the porch up for a three-year-old,
naked and muddy, who hands me a crushed

blossom. He says nothing. I thank him
and tuck the bloom into my book.

# Water Poem in a Time of War

The soap curls, eardrum-soft,
my body in the bath as easily

undone. Across the world,
two women soldiers blown

apart inside their armored car,
in the same country where

Shanidar 4, Neanderthal,
lay buried in a cave beneath

enough remains of seeds and
pollen to suggest a funeral.

Grape hyacinth and groundsel.
Woody horsetail. Yarrow.

Those hard bones,
that gentleness.

# On Kenosis

You dream you've had one kidney all your life.
And this is news to you.
Your hand moves to your lower back:
no pang to tell you that
you haven't had enough to drink.

The doctor shakes his head.
How could you have lived this way,
the hollow in your side
transforming nothing,

leaving waste to waste?
The lecturer on Francis of Assisi
says he lived "without a safety net," with joy.

Would not touch coins
or a spare robe for cold. Tell me,

what will you do with your secret poverty?

# To the Neighbors' Cut-down Trees

In two days, you vanished—no,
you didn't simply fade into the winter-
solstice light, all seven of you
city trees that drip your clustered
seeds and beetles mating twice a year
in chains of red and black, crunching
in the vacuum's maw as you did in
the chipping truck, you seven
long-limbed and untidy
beauties, standing still
in all your turgor when the man
who balanced in the cherry-picker
sawed you into logs, cradling
each one as if he meant it
for the fireplace—no, you fell
as I chopped onions in the kitchen
and the voices on the radio,
a Jewish mother and a Palestinian
whose son and brother had been lost
to gunfire, spoke of bearing
the same pain, you roared,
your bark sheared into
bits, refusing to die
quietly, leaving me
with rooflines, power-
lines and light
reminding
me I don't live
in the shady
and protecting
woods.

# Tea

A woman named Virginia
steeps her Mormon underclothes
so they won't show
under her sheer blouse,
so they'll soak up the forbidden
leaves (*hot drinks are not
for the body or belly*) and
grow dark against her skin,
becoming it, invisible.

I once dressed the body
of a Mormon woman
for her burial, pulled up
cotton stretched so thin from
living, it had almost
disappeared—what
was left of it so body-stained,
it pressed against her white
clay skin like leaves.

# Door Psalm

There are the doors
in and out of the world:
the white bed,
the prison gate,
the still pool, deeper than it looks,
the heart valve open or shut,
the mineshaft,
the stone rolled from the tomb.

There are the doors
of the body:
the mouth that accepts
the drink at last,
the womb that lets in
and lets out,
the eyelid that lifts
in recognition.

There are the doors
you see with an inner eye:
the moment you pull up
a flower and fear
the ground has opened for you;
the wind that enters your room
and asks you
to leave the life you know.

*How to Recognize a Lady*

Emma Bolden

"'A gentleman stands behind a *lady's* chair until she is seated,' but the use of it in conversation is very limited, unless we wish to imply our own humbler position . . . Remember, the King of England in his abdication speech referred to Wallis Simpson as 'the *woman* I love.' The word used properly has great dignity and meaning. A man, speaking of his wife, should refer to her as a 'woman' to his friends, as a 'lady' only to tradespeople and various others in service capacities. He may say to his new client, 'I'd like you to meet my wife sometime—a charming *woman.*' To the station porter he should say, 'Will you help the *lady* over there with the bags while I buy the tickets?'"

—*Amy Vanderbilt's Complete Book of Etiquette: A Guide to Gracious Living,* 1952

# How to Recognize a Lady

She writes this, Your Honor Dear Sirs Misters Gentlemen, to make acquaintance, haste, an answered inquiry.

She is the book of slander, a match dropped in dry glass.

She is a head sprouting snakes, milk for gall, low rolled smokes and poor taste. She is a cigarette's sizzle in gin, a two-lipped tattoo on his collar's starch.

She is the twelfth rib gone stray. She is the side stuck with whalebone stays. She hides herself, lacking a suitable silk. She scrubs her hands spotless when burning soft coal.

She is sorry, begs your pardon, mercy. She is a thumb stump on china, two footsoles slit clean.

She is not only proper but necessary. The Good Book balances her head. She is presented to old women thus: "Mrs. S——please meet Miss B——. Gladly." She is the neck's twig stretched out past snap. She prunes her right hand before offering, keeps scripture and blood quietly.

She is two knives at the banquet, blade slicing a sternum's strongbox. She keeps her work clean: mop, pail, and arm. Her skin shatters dishwater dry.

She is whipped to walk a straight line. She never eats unless hungry, never eats until full. She knows the front desk is no place to comb hair. In public, she keeps finger, pencils from her teeth.

She is as always honored to dance with you. She shall be delighted, glad, thrilled. She will be a skilled tongue, an obedient fist of petals, of rain.

She sends this by argon, by wing, by hoof against airstream, the sweat taste of sea. She seals this with perfume, with rouge, with asphalt, four fingers sliced clean, the lid of her lame eye.

She is As Always Sincerely Yours. She is Forever Found Truly Yours. She is Affectionately Yours. She begs to remain ever Your——. She hopes to receive favor, reply; she is Ever Indebtedly——.

# God Is in the Ceiling

Inside my bed I am
a good girl. I lie

still and careful,
keep limb from limb.

Outside I hear living.
Trees wave skeleton hands,

the moon's fingernail scratches
the far-cornered sky. I pray

*O Lord let me,* keep cool
as a clam's flesh. I am sick

with purity, with waiting
without the what for. Rain

rolls itself through
the gutters, birds flap off

their wings. The night keeps on
being night, and God

is a silent fissure, a slit
in the plaster's settling calm.

## Will and Testament

I come from a long line of pistols, hilts hefted in pearl-ringed hands.
My ancestors cut their teeth on nicked diamonds, stole furs from
velvet death beds. They lived on ether, horseflesh, spit. Their boots
wore seventeen sets of buttons. In photographs, they never fear the
blind that follows a flash. I come from a long line of unmarked
graves. By destiny, I am my own kind of thief. I steal wrecks and
windfalls, gloat over downed trees. I keep my racket tidy: one false
word, I'll nine-iron my own knees.

# The Established Household

Bedsheets curdled, the night came down
nearer and dearer (my God) for he, a snore
beside me, bored already.

Mothers and white magazines
urged *Anything's better*
*than alone*. I agreed. I wanted to be

the taste of one whole
flower in his mouth, the catch
in his voice when he said

*I need.*     I did what it took:
        I was a flesh fire in fishnets,
        a wet dream smoking French cigarettes.

        I was the baker, kneading out bread.
        I was mescaline sweat, the shine
        of a landscape's moonlit side, I was

nothing but body, raw,
all breast hip and thigh. What
he wanted, I made—less questions,

more lipstick, eggshell shards fished
from a yolk's yellow eye—want only
to be wanted, whatever the price.

# X

I was a yellow Emily, a gem of infinite forget. I was small and folded to fit tight corners. I was water-soluble, dissolved in a crinoline sea. The other girls wore their teeth like diamonds. They were pure dazzle, blinding luminosity. I wanted to grow curled from their scalps, to shine, one of three top coats of lacquer on their nails. They found my small kindnesses unacceptable. I pared my mouth down to knife's mirror, found fame by wounding with glimmer and glare.

# The Attempted Speaks

The first choice was not
my own. I wanted to be more
than accident, one hand
on the mirror, sheer gloss of breath
proven as steam.
I was however

never brave
and never sure. Hauled
by my own voice
out of that grave

which could have been dirt—
two red oaks for eyelids, fine
grass for thighs—

which could have been a hand
of blue light held forever

or nothing, all. I had already done
what I was advised. I asked
the sky for answers.
The sky said

rain, snow,
a wet lump of paper,
its words sneezed off.
The sky said

*What if your body*
*is an egg, what if when split*
*you'll slide out, yolk sheen*
*and shine.*

It was not
the revenge you assume,
one final crimson fit

thrown on the floor. It wasn't
an end but wanting

the light that passes      through sleep's windows
the voice heard from far      a clear word      forever
soft blue done of sky      *Requiem*
*æternam      lux perpetua luceat      requiescant*
*requiescant*
rest.

# Duet

*for Diann Blakely*


I drove an unstarred night, hands only
knowing where the car

was going, hands and not
me, as if inside of me there was

        that other girl whose face
        sliced a clean grin, who saw death

        was a gloved hand
        and held on:

                        *Tonight her angel doesn't show.*
      *Tonight she said enough    let me lead her through traffic*
                        *a fogged wash of red lights*

          *up the sky    the clouds and their great nothing*
               *but rain    the river caught crashing.*
            *By stop light    by starred light*

           *by the light of the cars that drive past*
               *I led her down to the river*
        *headlights shimmering the shift of waves*

          *take her in    take her under    away.*

My own body's snare,
that birdcage of bone,

a line of traffic
and then more traffic, tires,

hand flat against window glass.
I was motion, I was

foot over foot to the river's
green hem, the light on the lake

> *a silk evening gown smooth*     *glitter*
> *sheen over toes ankles calves*    *wanted again*
> *to be dressed*    *slid into the water a slip*

> *knees under*    *mirror trees*    *the moon*
> *in reverse*    *the deep shimmers light*    *the water*
> *easy to breathe*    *and only*

> *a red sweater on sand behind*
> *red face on a white field*    *surrender*
> *swallow*    *sink*    *this not*

Not the way I wanted.
Not eye sockets as snail shells, not

a blanket of mud, not jaw
rotted unlocked, tongue

a weed with no words. I wanted
to make myself someone

more than the long vanish, flesh silt,
a clear glow of bone, hand's flat

disappear. I wanted
to make myself up

from the depths, to rise,
to rise, to rise.

# The Unfinished Body

I wanted at last to live
honestly. Thinking it best

to start small, I told
the mailman I hated

his new self-stick stamps,
showed my uneven breasts

to the clerk at the mall.
Farther: I sold off a room

full of clothes, ran nude
through the city, sun-seared,

my skin a red lie. That too
I stripped, became the blue

bulge of muscle, blood-pumping
vein, itself a false dream

I could never believe. What
was true? A clear wave at morning,

a dress of stars at noon, at night
the edge where asphalt meets field.

# Fall

When I came to your body I spoke it, a language.
You were my tongue. When I came

to your body I knew it as not
even body—you were field, you were grasses

rolling themselves into distance. I knew you:
lake, prairie, moon a blank eye

overhead, sky overhead holding
its nosegay of stars. Or I

was not I, but a small sheep
in the wide field, trotting dumb

and glad towards the gleam
in your hand, happy to let you

lead me: your silver grin,
the hook sharpened.

## Courtships and Engagements

Marry a man with a hammer. Marry a man with a gold money clip, a medal from the rusted War. Marry a man with green spectacles, a sheep-skin balance sheet. Make sure to tap his teeth. If canines are of polished wood, discard and proceed. Keep your garters hooked, your purse hung straight. Cover your ankles from a wanderlust gaze. Marry a man who swallows lobster claws whole, fells age-old oaks with one stroke. Marry a man who'll thaw your cold nature, who'll force you to take it—a shot of rum, a public fist, a young dog's blood wet coat.

# The Confessional

Bless me Father for I have plucked
the smooth down from my wings
and fried them in oil, served them
to him on a fair Friday night.

An hour in the fan's hiss, my eye a keyhole
poised for his foot's fall. I slept nights
in the bathroom, trusted the lock
to keep its mouth shut.

My own mouth
wears a dull coat of moans.

The aftertaste of his thumb,
the dust on a family portrait.

I woke to the taste of Lysol.

I swear it was an accident.

I wish Goldilocks had been eaten.

I bare my teeth
at strangers. My right hand
does its job.

I cut off my hands and buried them.
They grew arms, torso, breasts, fresh
body, a pink skirt and heels. I let
her smile for me
and kneel.

# Duet (Reprise)

You can try
to lose me. Give it a year      a month
a night of trying to sleep and still waking

to night's empty eye. Finally      I am the pitch
that rises      bone upon bone until
flesh      until you      until the song

that shores you back
to the river's edge      hands glad
with the weight of stone.

I tell you      Death be not
but a little sting      the smooth
red sailing away.

# *Translating a Bridge*

## Vivian Teter

# "every Spark is numbered"

On scraps, over backs
and sides of torn
squares, pinned
into fold of dress
or tucked down
pocket, delivered
in secret—
*Open me carefully*
Emily writes
to her sweet muse.

Dropping
task at hand, stopping
to catch the quick
appearance, quicker
retreat of vision or
image, igniting
missive after
missive in
hot assault,
full pursuit sent
burning over
snowy fields
or blazing through
New England June—

the poet's body
breaking into
fiery verb
singing to one
of similar
essence—

passion for one
sparking
passion for
all the world,
its many daily
dark or bright
amazements:

"O One I cannot love enough
O One beyond all touch:
I will then seduce
your soul, delight
your mind—my words
will surpass those of any,
each verse asking
faithfully to the last
*Will you*
*wholly be mine,*
each stanza answering
faithfully
to the last, *You will*

I will write *yes* and
*yes* over and
over, each line
shaping you
immortal, making you
divine, divinely Mine:
Love, Beloved, Lovely
Only One, Only World:
my slashes and syllables
stand bold, unbreakable
against any Zero
for all time."

# Translating a Bridge

Damn in-the-dark     scratch
      & handscrawl.

    Is it
        *salve* or *salvage?*

    *Seek, seeking,* or
        *singing?*

      Hurry to translate
   at brink of
day.

# After the Fire Experiments

Francis Bacon, *Novum Organum*

Finally we went outside and saw
the burning world.
So much we had to touch:
the skin of any animal, its carcass.
From hair, from feathers, we drew flame,
from reeds, straw, dried leaves.
The nature of heat
became our obsession.

A horse we saw, stopped along the road,
stood luminous in sweat.
Wood rotting shone in the dark.
We wanted to know: what secret remains
when layer after layer
the fleshly apparitions
fall away?

We had not guessed there was so much fire.
We journeyed to the shore, listened
to the sailors, how in the East
women weave down into wrapping,
the feathers for decades generating warmth.
Under our oars the sea glittered.
Never again would we conceive fire singular
and clear, the very word
close to meaningless
for all that we saw.

When will our hearts burst into red dust?
All night we dream the back of God
on fire.

And roses: packed in baskets,
bruised together, even these often catch flame.

# Hunger of No Tongue

After July boils then breaks
you begin, you journey weekly out to the tree,
thumb and forefinger pressing to check
for a give in fig-flesh, eyes checking
to see the bitter vanish from taut green skin.

You return—they cling to the branch. August
heaves overhead. You return—they glitter after rain
like haughty emeralds safe from speech.
Even the birds have not come.
September swells and crests. This time

you step in among the branches,
you search from inside for any sign.
The big leaves, hands of five swollen thumbs
wave in wind, yellow, and fall.
October, and then you see:

you see it all:

quickly from stark
branches you tear
one after
the other, a far

faded memory of seeds deep
in pink-red flesh deepens
that pain dead between your eyes:
*such flesh, ripened, easily falls away.*

The lesson sears
your brain. You bear down hard,
tooth toward tooth:
Lost, you eat them green.

# Meditation on "Tok," the Dinka Word for "One"

*For Dut Akech, who spoke of crossing the Gilo River under
fire from troops on both sides while many other Lost Boys of
Sudan who couldn't swim begged for his help*

If I could delete the memory
if I could wash it from your mind, if I could sweep it
over the edge of the planet far out into space
and let the stars blow out in horror

If I could break the clock, if I could yank its hands
back 20 ruthless years, if I could build dam after dam
and back up time's river to 1986     before Kenya, before Ethiopia
before Gilo, before all of it     if I could

vanish the soldiers     dry up the river     return your mother
and father     and brothers     to you
your village
every house, every cow, every stalk of sorghum and the calm

wind and the sweet dripping of peace—
You are not 25. You have suffered beyond time
back beyond any counting of days to the first time
a man picked up a stone and struck the skull of his brother's

boy, to the first twist, urge, fear: first thought
of grinding the seed of a fellow human into extinction.
You have walked through centuries of pain
through a world where adults slaughter children

and human life weighs nothing on the scale
of riches for a few.
I cannot tell you what it is that broke inside
when I heard the heaviness and ache

the unspeakable unsaid behind your words
that was clearly said in your very breath and breathless
pause of grief.
I can only tell you I *yearn* (the word we learned this morning)

I yearn for the healing of those wounds that howl through your nights
and I can tell you there are many more like me, growing in number
we who have had enough centuries of weeping and bandaging
*after* we let those wielding death have their way

we who have had enough centuries to know
it is past time to stop the slashing and drilling of flesh
the wounding and extraction of the human heart—
not theirs, not ours—for there is only One

human heart undivided by borders and markets.

Teach me from your language the Dinka words
for *one* and *we*—
*one* as in "one indivisible," *one* as in
before counting and adding, possession and accumulation

and teach me *we* as in "we" before the lie of separation
before any Other that betrayed
and destroyed its own kind, the "we" that is indestructible
the "we" that can reach, can see    through the delusion of "I."

Dut, we share only one heart and it beats for a world more just
and for a turning back from the brink.
It beats an uncrushable, unstarvable music
a ceaseless music that flows through all tribes and peoples

and that just might, in the end, rise up and pull us all
from our rapid, collective falling.

# Those in the Photos

*In memory of Li Chunmei*

The children dreamed
they were the blood

that shrank into
the earth, traveled

up root through trunk
and made the trees

swell and break
into fiery leaves:

red birds walking
over the new snow.

# Red-Winged Blackbird

*For Medo Bangura & The Refugee All Stars*

a gash of blood,
brushstroke of gold,
you wear these gifts
like hard-won epaulettes

each not two shades, but one:
one band of flaming pain
issuing a balm
of light—

Who can say where or when
anguish twists and lifts,
honey dropping then
to feed the soul forward . . .

We come out the other side,
know only
in glancing
back:

what to eye and brain
won't give way,
to heart and hand
will part. Quick,

gather your colors, keep
a steady flight
through the black knives
of the night.

# Across the Street All Autumn

When the days bring
no schedule
other than medications

When getting dressed
—that alone—shows the soul's
embrace of the failing body

When no one visits
and you sit in your lawn chair
under the tulip poplar

gazing darkly then shyly
at the edges of a blue sky
quizzical in its brilliance:

the sun itself praises you
the wind (old nuzzler) comes close

morning unfolds a quilt frayed but bright
with late summer threads

and the leaves begin to hum
in their going

drowning the growl of a distant machine
and dropping low, golden vowels all around you

intimate
but indecipherable

as that first letter opened long ago
then folded close at heart

and then carried
this far.

# An Explanation of the Rain

*We ca ke leech* (Thank you) *Lost Boys*

In those last moments,
no longer able to walk
or to swallow,
I will see the four of us

huddling and laughing
in a cold spring rain.
Dut like a tall, thin sapling
holds the umbrella

high above us all while William sings,
shining and threading each rescued
Dinka word into a sturdy wrap
that circles our shoulders brightly.

Bul then turns to explain:
"We walked many, many miles
many, many months—bush, desert
—best was rain. You see,

between us and those dead, just
one leaf to eat, just one hand of mud.
And now you see us here—a new land—
now we are not having to drink this rain!"

How your onyx skin gleamed wetly
young men of Sudan, lighting that gray sky!
When I lie waiting, face-up in final thirst
it's this memory I'll taste

and your laughter I'll see, glistening,
as my body becomes the language of rain.

# Last Dance

Let me at least sit back up
for this one, knocking the atoms
of the coffin awry, de-connecting
a collar bone, dropping a hip,
tossing wrist to sky and slipping
clean through this old costume
I've sorely outgrown. Let me
learn the steps as I go—
no flesh to fool us, no panting
and moaning, no words between—
just the beat, without the bloody heart.
Grab me by the gleam this time,
the silver swing of soul unhinged
and baby, blast: blast through
gravity, tear up time, nuke
this dull earthly dish
Let me shine and rise
Let me ride the blue-gold pulse
of the universe divine
Beam me up, bounce me out
Warp me in, swing me through
Anything but dark
Anywhere but down
neutrons humming loose
protons sparking apart
electrons ringing
something new
High and light
Shimmer and flow
Sing it loud now
Pulse it on out
Oh sweet black honey
eternity on your hands
you done, finally,
this time
got it
all
so
right.

# Tulip for a New Millennium

*Find what way,* you sing,
*we each are made to catch and release*

(like your tight cup of petals)
*more, oh more, long-needed light*

after all the torn, wounded
centuries under all those darkly wed

to themselves, to Self only, while we waited
while we wept and sang, dear tulip, we who

once lived lost in your beauty: we
are no longer so tender or weak

we hear and feel now the desperate red
whip of the ache of this time:

and together, just now possible:
together what we gather—syllable

brush stroke, bold note swelling
and sailing over and through—

what we make and gather enough
at last, an ocean against all rivers

dark and void, this ocean greater
gracing hands that open and release

image after image over the mass
graves and palaces of history and out onto

a dazzling plain (*far, near*) where finally
we walk, weaponless and unafraid.

# Two Last Reasons for Words

### I.

Sophora japonica
            (pagoda tree cascading
                    your tiny lanterns
            of lit green seeds
late in the day
        this windy end
of November)

how will we ever
        sufficiently
                adore
                    you?

### II.

Hawthorn      just off the path

        flashing    hundreds and hundreds of red berries

        clustered on dark
    bare branches      all tussling with wind

and then      (*what's this?*)      five white
petals      (*two tattered*)      of one last
            blossom
        (*impossible!*) just      thrusting
                    into December so brazenly
                        holding out that pollen like that—

    Sweet Being (*brilliant
against gray sky*)      there is always time

            (*always!*)      to open
                        to flame.

# Notes

## About the Authors

# NOTES

BOLDEN: "How to Recognize a Lady" is inspired by and incorporates information from Mary E. Clark and Margery C. Quigley's *Etiquette, Jr.*

"The Established Household" and "Courtships and Engagements" owe their titles to *Amy Vanderbilt's Complete Book of Etiquette: A Guide to Gracious Living.*

"The Attempted Speaks": The Latin, adapted from the Requiem Mass, translates as *Let perpetual light illuminate eternal rest, let them rest.*

HART: "On Kenosis": Kenosis: Greek (theological) *self-emptying.*

TETER: "Meditation on 'Tok'": In 1986, when the Lost Boys were 4 to 7, Sudanese government forces destroyed their villages and left most of them orphaned. Tens of thousands crossed Sudan on foot to U.N. camps in Ethiopia, only to be forced, after a regime change, back into Sudan via the crocodile-infested Gilo River. Those who survived walked hundreds of miles to camps in Kenya and were warehoused there for 12 years. In 2001, the State Department brought 3800 to the U.S. The Lost Boys regard the genocide in Darfur as an extension of the destruction of their southern Sudan homeland.

"Those in the Photos": Li Chunmei (*Washington Post* 5/13/02) was employed at 12 cents an hour as a runner in a toy factory in Songgang, China. In the peak pre-Christmas season, she died after working 16-hour shifts for 60 days straight. Her roommates found her on the factory dorm's bathroom floor, bleeding from the mouth and nose. She had wanted to return to her father's farm.

"Red-Winged Blackbird": Sierra Leone's Refugee All Stars began writing songs in 1997 to comfort fellow citizens who fled from war to refugee in camps in Guinea. Medo Bangura, after being forced at gunpoint to kill his infant son during the war, stopped playing with the band for a time. He recently found the spirit to continue, explaining, "The only way I can live here is by playing with this band."

# ABOUT THE AUTHORS

EMMA BOLDEN is a poet, playwright, and fiction writer whose work has appeared in *VERSE, MARGIE, Spoon River Poetry Review,* and other journals. She's won awards from Alabama Writer's Forum, American Theatre Co-op, *Georgetown Review,* and New England Writers. She holds a BA from Sarah Lawrence College and MFA from the University of North Carolina at Wilmington. She teaches English at Auburn University.

GLADYS JUSTIN CARR, a former Nicholson Fellow at Smith College and University Fellow at Cornell, left her day job as a publishing executive with McGraw Hill and HarperCollins to write full time. Her work has been cited in *Literary Magazine Review,* and has appeared in over fifty publications including *North Atlantic Review, Meridian Anthology of Contemporary Poetry, The New York Times, South Carolina Review, Potomac Review* and *Worcester Review.*

HEIDI HART, author of the memoir *Grace Notes: The Waking of a Woman's Voice* (University of Utah Press, 2004), a finalist for the Utah Book Award, also received a 2007 Utah Arts Council grant for a book-length essay project. Other poems and essays have appeared in *Northern Lights, Quarterly West, Cimarron Review, Lumina,* and *Pilgrimage.* A musician as well as a writer, she is in training to provide harp and vocal music for the dying.

VIVIAN TETER, professor of English at Virginia Wesleyan College in Norfolk, VA, holds a BA from Hollins University and an MFA from the University of Arizona. Her work has appeared in *The Missouri Review, Poetry East, Jabberwock, Green Mountains Review,* and other journals. She has been awarded residencies at The Virginia Center for the Creative Arts and Byrdcliffe Artists Colony.

# ABOUT THE BOOK

green press
INITIATIVE

Toadlily Press is committed to preserving ancient forests and natural resources. We elected to print *Edge by Edge* on 50% post consumer recycled paper, processed chlorine free. As a result, for this printing, we have saved:

2  Trees (40' tall and 6-8" diameter)
670  Gallons of Wastewater
270  Kilowatt Hours of Electricity
74  Pounds of Solid Waste
145  Pounds of Greenhouse Gases

Toadlily Press made this paper choice because our printer, Thomson-Shore, Inc., is a member of Green Press Initiative, a nonprofit program dedicated to supporting authors, publishers, and suppliers in their efforts to reduce their use of fiber obtained from endangered forests.

For more information, visit www.greenpressinitiative.org

*Edge by Edge* was composed in Sabon, a typeface designed in 1967 at Linotype by Jan Tschichold. The type family—a classic, elegant and highly legible book face—is based on the work of Claude Garamond and his pupil Jacques Sabon.